SONGS

OF AMERICAN FOLKS

Satis N. Coleman and Adolph Bregman

Illustrated by Alanson Hewes

Granger Index Reprint Series

BOOKS FOR LIBRARIES PRESS
FREEPORT, NEW YORK

Dedicated to the best of friends
and the most generous of critics

Elsie O. Bregman

Acknowledgment

The compilation of this book has been one of my least arduous tasks. Aside from the obviously great pleasure of such an undertaking, the work was really done for me by the many friends from whom the songs were learned, and whose contributions thereby really made up the book. To these friends, the acknowledgments made with each song will, I hope, indicate the very deep gratitude I feel for each and every one.

But my obligation is no less great to the many friends whose company on innumerable occasions has called forth these songs; those warm audiences whose sympathetic understanding and unstinted appreciation have been a most important factor in the growth of this collection.

And this note would be wholly inadequate without expression of my rare pleasure in the accompaniments composed by my associate, Mrs. Satis N. Coleman. As in no other collection that I have ever seen, these arrangements have caught the naïveté, the wide-eyed innocence, and at the same time the terse directness and downright honesty of these folk tunes. This book would have been impossible without them.

A. B.

Preface

Until a comparatively few years ago, American folk songs formed a class of music known only to "folks"—old-fashioned people—and to a very small group of musicians who appreciated their charm. Today, however, thanks to the work of Lomax, Weldon Johnson, Scarborough, Sandburg, Niles, and many others, folk songs have achieved impressive distinction in our literature. They are loved for the innocence and artlessness of their music, for their simple beauty as literature, and they are beginning to be appreciated for their high educational value as direct and living reflections of the many facets of American history.

It is not the purpose of the present book to be complete or all-embracing. Rather, it is meant to be a sampling, a representative choosing, of authentic American songs that represent the "folk" element, and that are *good to sing.* Most of them are not too well known, having appeared in few, if any, other collections of similar nature, and the versions given here are quite different from many of those to be found elsewhere.

These songs were not really "collected." They have accrued almost without intention or design. They are unlooked-for dividends of a certain number of years of living, a certain number of places lived in, a certain need and habit of singing under the "right" conditions—good company and a light heart. They are all indigenous to the United States; all were learned from people who live here. To be sure, many of the songs originated in other countries—but so did countless good Americans! They have accumulated in many ways, from many places; incomplete, fragmentary, a verse, a bar, with gaps filled in by accidents of time and place. A line of a song was first heard in a Colorado mine to the beat of a hammer and drill. Two decades later, two thousand miles away, within these same United States, the missing verses were conjured up at a party, by a mellow guitar.

A knowledge of the spontaneous songs of the "plain" people is necessary for the complete understanding of any nation. Natural peoples are impelled to express their deepest feelings in song. They sing of their joys, sorrows, and tragedies; their loves, fears, and religious aspirations. And in their songs are revealed their customs, their language, their ways of living, working, and playing, as well as their deepest emotions.

One of the greatest fields of usefulness for these songs is with boys and girls of high-school age. Many of the songs given here have been used with gratifying success in both the Junior High and Senior High divisions of the Lincoln School of Columbia University. Most adolescents have grown tired of "children's songs," but they do not yet have the maturity of purpose or the patience for the drill necessary to perfect a large repertoire of songs that are usually considered "the best" in music literature. This may come to them later on—*provided* their love of singing is sustained through these restless years by a generous inclusion of songs that are merely *fun to sing.*

The junior high school brings more problems to the music teacher than any other section of the school. These boys and girls are just entering into a real appreciation of the emotional lives of human beings. "The Golden Willow Tree," for instance, strikes at the heart of the junior high school boy in a way that he cannot explain in words. The over-stressed tragedy in "Blood on the Saddle" touches off his sense of the ridiculous. This and others give him opportunity to satisfy his innate need for nonsense.

With the voice limitations of the adolescent and the average untrained singer in mind, most of the songs have been set in a low key, for ease in singing.

The first verse of each song is set with the music. The succeeding verses are set apart on the facing pages. This separation has been deliberate. The meter in folk songs is often irregular. To "cue" into the melody the extra notes for the extra words that may occur from verse to verse would destroy the simplicity of the score and make it difficult to read. Moreover, it is not in keeping with the nature of such songs to have the words of every verse rigidly set to the tune. Each singer of folk songs will sing the words as he feels them, making the adjustments to the tune as they seem best to him.

It is suggested that the tune be well learned in the beginning, as set to the first verse. If another verse has an extra word or two in the line, hum the tune for that line, and see where a note must be doubled. If a line has fewer words than the tune calls for, then slur two or more notes to one word until it seems to fit.

We commend these songs to all ages. They are good for both old and young because they are fun to sing, and because they tell of the rise of America accurately, simply, and inimitably. Some of them, such as "The Frog and the Mouse," and "The Fox Went Through the Town, Oh!" will be enjoyed even by the youngest singers, while children of seven or eight, and older, will appreciate "The Night-Herding Song" and "Run, Nigger, Run"; and adults will select according to the mood of the moment.

S. N. C.
A. B.

8

Contents

When the Land Was Young

Most of these songs came to us from the Old Country—England and Scotland. They may be couched in archaic English; they may speak of pounds and pence. Yet today, after more than three hundred years, they are still sung and loved here. They took root firmly and acquired full citizenship; they are now American.

The Fox Went Through the Town, Oh!

*Even today a current English folk song, it was brought to New York
by Mrs. Katherine B. Peeples from Bedford County, Va., where it
had flourished in the following version. It was generously given to
the writer for a birthday present!*

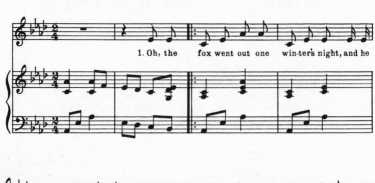

1. Oh, the fox went out one win-ter's night, and he

played to the moon to give him light, for he had man-y miles to go that night, be-

fore he reached the town, Oh! town Oh! town Oh! For he had man-y miles to

go that night, be - fore he reached the   town, Oh!

Last verse ends here

2. At last he came to the farmer's yard,
   And the ducks and the geese were all agog.
   "Oh, one of you shall grease my be-ard,
   "Before I leave the town, Oh!"
   Town Oh! Town Oh!
   "One of you shall grease my be-ard,
   "Before I leave the town, Oh!"

3. Old Mother Woggle Goggle jumped out of bed,
   Ran to the window and poked out her head.
   "John, John, John, the black duck's gone,
   "The fox went through the town, Oh!"
   Town Oh! Town Oh!
   "John, John, John, the black duck's gone,
   "The fox went through the town, Oh!"

4. John jumped out of bed and he run up the hill,
   And he piped and he piped both clear and shrill.
   Methinks I hear the echo still,
   The fox went through the town, Oh!
   Town Oh! Town Oh!
   Methinks I hear the echo still,
   The fox went through the town, Oh!

Gay Jemmie, the Miller

*Here is one of our very early songs—pre-Revolution. Its origin—
perhaps England, but very likely America. It has the flavor of New
England where it was found by Helen Hartness Flanders, as pub-
lished in her* VERMONT FOLK SONGS AND BALLADS.

1. Gay Jem-mie, the mil-ler, went court-ing of late, To a rich farm-er's
daugh-ter called "Beau-ti-ful Kate." She had for her por-tion gay
jew-els and rings, She had for her por-tion full fif-ty fine things; She

had for her por-tion gay jewels and gowns; She had for her por-tion, She

had for her por-tion, She had for her por-tion full five thou-sand pounds.

2. The day was appointed, the money laid down,
Which proved the full value of five thousand pound.
The parson was sent for, the couple were met.
Said Jem to the farmer, "I've one more regret.
"Although your daughter is lovely and fair,
    "I can't have your daughter,
    "I can't have your daughter,
"I can't have your daughter without your gray mare!"

3. The money soon vanished clean out of his sight
And likewise Miss Katie, his joy and delight.
And then like a dog he was kicked out the door,
And ordered never to come there no more.
Then Jemmie he tore at his long yellow hair,
    And wished he had never,
    And wished he had never,
And wished he had never stood for the gray mare.

4. A year or two later, that's just about right,
He chanced to meet Katie, his joy and delight.
"How are you, Miss Katie, and don't you know me?"
"I seem to remember, I've met you," said she,
"Or somebody like you with long yellow hair,
    "Who once came a-courting,
    "Who once came a-courting,
"Who once came a-courting my father's gray mare!"

The Golden Willow Tree

A ballad harking from the days of Queen Elizabeth, which has pervaded folk singing from that day to this. The present version came to us by way of Desmond Powell, but it is close kin to "The Lowlands Low," and "The Golden Vanitie," and related to a score of others which carry the refrain, "Lowlands low" or "Lowlands alone."

1. 'Twas just as dawn rose o'er the North Sea,

Close at an-chor lay the Gold-en Wil-low Tree, And she lay in the Low-lands,

lone-some, a-lone, She lay in the Low-lands, a-lone. -lone.

16

2. 'Twas just as dawn rose o'er the North Sea,
   There came upon her the Turkish Reveille,
   As she lay in the Lowlands, lonesome alone,
   She lay in the Lowlands alone.

3. Then up spoke the Captain, said "What shall we do?
   "We can't flee them, so swift will they pursue,
   "And they'll sink us in the Lowlands, lonesome alone,
   "Sink us in the Lowlands alone."

4. Then up spoke the cabin boy, said "What will you give me
   "If I send her to the bottom of the cold North Sea?
   "For I'll sink her in the Lowlands, lonesome alone,
   "Sink her in the Lowlands alone."

5. "Oh, I'll give you gold, and I'll make you free,
   "And my eldest, eldest daughter, your wedded wife shall be,
   "If you'll sink her in the Lowlands, lonesome alone,
   "Sink her in the Lowlands alone."

6. Then he swam through the water with tools made to fit,
   And he bored nine holes in the bottom of the ship,
   And he sank her in the Lowlands, lonesome alone,
   Sank her in the Lowlands alone.

7. Some with their coats and some with their caps,
   Tried to stop up the salt-water gaps.
   But they sank in the Lowlands, lonesome alone,
   Sank in the Lowlands alone.

8. O Captain, O Captain, be a man of your word,
   "Throw me a rope and take me on board,
   "For I've sunk her in the Lowlands, lonesome alone,
   "Sunk her in the Lowlands alone."

9. "Oh, I won't give you gold and I won't make you free,
   "And my eldest, eldest daughter your wedded wife won't be,
   "Though you've sunk her in the Lowlands, lonesome alone,
   "Sunk her in the Lowlands alone."

10. Then he threw up his hands, and a prayer breathed he,
    And he sank to the bottom of the cold North Sea,
    And his ghost haunts the Lowlands, lonesome alone,
    His ghost haunts the Lowlands alone.

Springfield Mountain

Originally a ballad serious in character, "Springfield Mountain"
dates back to before 1776. By the nineteenth century it had become
a "comic" in a variety of versions of which the following is probably
the best known.

1. On Spring-field Moun-tain there did dwell a love-ly

youth, I knew him well. Too roo de noo, too roo de

Left hand octave higher.......

nay; Too roo de noo, too roo de nay.

8va..................

18

2. This lovely youth one day did go
   Down to the meadow for to mow.

   Chorus: Too roo, etc.

3. He had not mowed quite round the field,
   When a pizen sarpint bit his heel.

   Chorus: Too roo, etc.

4. They took him back to Mollie dear,
   Which made her feel so very queer.

   Chorus: Too roo, etc.

5. Now Mollie had two ruby lips,
   With which the pizen she did sip.

   Chorus: Too roo, etc.

6. Now Mollie had a hollow tooth,
   And so the pizen killed them both.

   Chorus: Too roo, etc.

7. Now lovers all this warning take:
   Oh, shun the bite of the pizen snake.

   Chorus: Too roo, etc.

The Frog and the Mouse

The Frog and the Mouse come of ancient and honorable lineage. They have been celebrated in song for centuries in a dozen versions and a hundred stanzas. The present version is said to have come from West Virginia, by J. H. Cox in FOLK SONGS OF THE SOUTH.

1. Frog went a-court-in', he did ride, Mmm-hm-m,

Frog went a-court-in', he did ride, Mmm-hm-m,

Frog went a-court-in', he did ride, With a sword and pis-tol by his side, Mmm-

Last verse ends

hm-m.

here

2. He went to Miss Mousie's den,
      Mmm hm-m
   He went to Miss Mousie's den,
      Mmm hm-m
   He went to Miss Mousie's den,
   And said, "Miss Mouse, is you
      within?"
      Mmm hm-m

3. "Yes sir, yes sir, I am in."
      Mmm hm-m
   "Yes sir, yes sir, I am in,"
      Mmm hm-m
   "Yes sir, yes sir, I am in.
   "Jus' lif' the latch an' walk right in!"
      Mmm hm-m

4. He took Miss Mousie on his knee,
      Mmm hm-m
   He took Miss Mousie on his knee,
      Mmm hm-m
   He took Miss Mousie on his knee,
   And said, "Miss Mouse, will you
      marry me?"
      Mmm hm-m

5. "Not without Uncle Rat's consent,"
      Umph-humph*
   "Not without Uncle Rat's consent,"
      Umph-humph
   "Not without Uncle Rat's consent,
   "I wouldn' marry the President."
      Umph-humph

6. At last Uncle Rat, he came home,
      Mmm hm-m
   At last Uncle Rat, he came home,
      Mmm hm-m
   At last Uncle Rat, he came home,
   Said, "Who been here sence I been
      gone?"
      Mmm hm-m

7. "The nices' man you ever see,"
      Mmm hm-m
   "The nices' man you ever see,"
      Mmm hm-m
   "The nices' man you ever see,"
   "And says he wants to marry me."
      Mmm hm-m

8. Uncle Rat he laugh' till he shook
      his fat side,
      Mmm hm-m
   Uncle Rat he laugh' till he shook
      his fat side,
      Mmm hm-m
   Uncle Rat he laugh' till he shook
      his fat side,
   To think of his little niece a bride.
      Mmm hm-m

9. Uncle Rat give his consent,
      Mmm hm-m
   Uncle Rat give his consent,
      Mmm hm-m
   Uncle Rat give his consent,
   An' the weasel wrote the publish-
      ment.
      Mmm hm-m

* Meaning "Oh, no!"

(*Additional verses on following page*)

10. Where shall the weddin' supper be?
    Mmm hm-m
    Where shall the weddin' supper be?
    Mmm hm-m
    Where shall the weddin' supper be?
    Down in the holler of a old oak tree.
    Mmm hm-m

11. First to come was a little brown bug,
    Mmm hm-m
    First to come was a little brown bug,
    Mmm hm-m
    First to come was a little brown bug.
    He drowned hisself in a 'lasses jug.
    Mmm hm-m

12. Nex' come in was a little wee fly,
    Mmm hm-m
    Nex' come in was a little wee fly,
    Mmm hm-m
    Nex' come in was a little wee fly.
    He ate so much he almos' die.
    Mmm hm-m

13. Next one in was a bumble bee,
    Mmm hm-m
    Next one in was a bumble bee,
    Mmm hm-m
    Next one in was a bumble bee,
    Carryin' a fiddle on his knee.
    Mmm hm-m

14. Las' to come was a big black dog,
    Mmm hm-m
    Las' to come was a big black dog,
    Mmm hm-m
    Las' to come was a big black dog.
    He chase' Miss Mousie up a holler
      log.
    Mmm hm-m

15. Sword and pistol on the shelf,
    Mmm hm-m
    Sword and pistol on the shelf,
    Mmm hm-m
    Sword and pistol on the shelf,
    If you want any more you'll have
      to sing it yourself.
    Mmm hm-m

Up and Down the Country

From New York to California—from Minnesota to Texas—we could list a thousand songs of Country Folks. They are endless—and they are good. Here are a chosen few.

Great-Granddad

The granddad of all pioneers, the first to settle the frontier, was a great legendary hero, and rightly so. He carved out his niche in the wilderness so that his boys could begin with a good foothold and continue to build higher and broader. His methods were simple—but it took Granddad to apply them! The present version was written by Jack Lambert and sung to us by Tex Ritter.

Rather fast

1. Great-grand-dad, when the land was young,
Barred his door with the wagon tongue; For the times was rough, an' the
red-skins mocked, An' he said his prayers with his shot-gun cocked.

2. He was a citizen, tough and grim;
   Danger was duck soup to him;
   He ate corn pone an' bacon fat.
   Great-grandson would starve on that.

3. Twenty-one children came to bless
   Granddad's home in the wilderness;
   Twenty-one boys but he didn't lose heart,
   For the dogs hunted rabbits an' they ketched right smart!

4. Twenty-one boys, an' how they grew,
   Tall an' strong on the bacon too.
   They hunted all day in their coonskin hats,
   An' slept all night with the dogs an' cats.

5. Twenty-one boys an' not one bad;
   They never got fresh with great-granddad,
   For if they had he'd a' been right glad
   To tan their hides with a hick'ry gad!

6. They grew strong in heart an' hand,
   Firm foundation of our land;
   Twenty-one boys an' a great-grandson—
   An' he has a terrible time with one!

Kansas Boys

*Sage advice from mothers to daughters, which, in the main, they dis-
regarded! Sandburg says that folks moving from Kentucky probably
took this song to Kansas, but from there on it has traveled in all
directions via thousands of willing helpers.*

1. Come a-long, girls, listen to my voice,

Don't you nev-er mar-ry no Kan-sas boys. If you do, your

fate will be, Hoe-cake, hom-i-ny and sass-a-fras tea.

2. They'll take you out on a jet black hill,
   Take you there against your will.
   Keep you there to perish on the plains;
   That's the way with the Kansas range.

3. When a young man falls in love,
   First its honey, then turtle dove.
   After he's married, no such thing:
   "Get up and get my breakfast, you good-for-nothin' thing!"

4. When they go to milk, they milk in a gourd,
   Leave it in a corner and cover with a board.
   Some get little—some get none;
   That's the way with the Kansas run.

5. When they go to meetin', the clothes they wear
   Is an old brown coat all picked and bare,
   An old white hat more rim than crown,
   A pair of cotton socks they wore the month aroun'.

Old Dan Tucker

Dan Emmett, a truly great writer of songs, made this ditty in 1830, and, even though it has undergone some changes over a century, it still remains one of the most loved and best remembered of the old minstrels' repertoire. For the version below we have to thank Burl Ives, a folk-song minstrel extraordinary of today.

1. Ah come to town de ud-der night, Ah

heard de noise, den saw de fight, De watch-man wuz a-

run-nin' 'roun' Cry-in' "Ol' Dan Tuck-er's come to town!"

2. Ol' Dan Tucker wus a mighty man;
   He washed 'is face in a fryin' pan,
   Combed 'is hair wid a wagon wheel,
   An' died wid de toothache in 'is heel.

   Chorus: So git out de way, etc.

3. Ol' Dan Tucker, he got drunk,
   He fell in de fire an' he kicked up a chunk.
   De red hot coals got in 'is shoe
   An' whee-ee! how de ashes flew!

   Chorus: So git out de way, etc.

Sweet Betsy from Pike

This is a song of the Gold Rush in the 1850's to California, and the one that seems to have outlived all the others, as well as the Gold Rushers themselves. It was a favorite wagon song.

Not too slow

1. Oh, don't you re-mem-ber sweet Bet-sy from Pike, Who

crossed the big moun-tains with her lov-er, Ike, With two yoke of cat-tle, a

large yel-low dog, A tall Shanghai roos-ter, and one spot-ted hog.

Chorus

Oh good-by, Pike Coun-ty, Fare-well for a while; We'll come back a-gain when we've panned out our pile.

2. They soon reached the desert, where Betsy gave out,
And down in the sand she lay rolling about;
While Ike, in great tears, looked on in surprise,
Saying, "Betsy, get up; you'll get sand in your eyes."

Chorus: Oh good-by, Pike County, etc.

3. The Shanghai run off and the cattle all died;
The last piece of bacon that morning was fried.
Poor Ike got discouraged, and Betsy got mad;
The dog wagged his tail and looked wonderful sad.

Chorus: Oh good-by, Pike County, etc.

4. One morning they climbed up a very high hill,
And with wonder looked down into old Placerville;
Ike shouted and said, as he cast his eyes down,
"Sweet Betsy, my darling, we've got to Hangtown!"

Chorus: Oh good-by, Pike County, etc.

The Lane County Bachelor

The early American homesteaders—real pioneers if ever there were any—have been celebrated in history and literature for over a century. But never has a more concise, crisp and vivid description been penned than in this song, which tells of one who couldn't "stick it out" for the five years needed to acquire full title to his land. And who is to say that he is not more deserving of sympathy than blame?

1. My name is Frank Bo - lar, 'n ol' bach-'lor I am, I'm a
My house it is built of the na - tion - al soil, An' the

keep-in' ole bach on a el - e-gant plan. You will find me out West in the
walls are e - rect-ed ac - cord-in' to Hoyle; An' the roof has no pitch, but it's

Coun-ty of Lane, Starv-in' to death on a Gov-ern-ment claim.
lev - el an' plain, An' I al - ways get wet when it hap-pens to rain.

32

Chorus

But hur - rah for Lane Coun - ty the Land of the Free, The home of the grass - hop - per, bed - bug an' flea, Oh, I'll sing loud her prais - es an' boast of her fame, Starv - in' to death on my Gov - ern - ment claim.

(Additional verses on following page)

33

2. How happy am I when I crawl into bed,
   An' a rattlesnake rattles his tail at my head,
   An' the gay little centipede, void of all fear,
   Crawls over my pillow and into my ear.
   An' the sweet little bedbug, merry an' bright,
   Keeps me a-scratchin' full half o' the night,
   An' the gay little louse with toes sharp as a tack
   Plays "Why don't you ketch me?" all over my back.

   Chorus: But hurrah for Lane County, the land of the blest,
   Where the farmers and laborers are always at rest,
   Where you've nothing to do but sweetly remain,
   An' starve like a man on your Government claim.

3. How happy am I on my Government claim,
   Where I've nothin' to lose, nothin' to gain,
   Nothin' to eat, nothin' to wear.
   Well, nothin' from nothin' is honest and square!
   But here I am stuck, an' here I mus' stay;
   My money's all gone an' I can't get away.
   Oh, there's nothin' will make a man hard and profane
   Like starvin' to death on a Government claim.

   Chorus: Then farewell to Lane County, farewell to the West.
   I'll go back to the land that I love best;
   I'll go back to Missouri an' get me a wife,
   An' live on corn dodgers the rest of my life.

Ridin' High, Wide an' Handsome

That most engaging individual, the roistering, hard-working, hard-playing, hard-living, and hard-dying cowboy has developed song which, like himself, is like unto no other. It ranges from the earth to the hereafter, and from deep misery to the lightest of hearts. It tells of a social being, but essentially a lone man, really happy only where people are few and spaces are wide.

Blood on the Saddle

*As told us by Tex Ritter, the tune originated among the cowboys at
Wickenburg, Arizona, and the words of the song were written at
Florence, Arizona, by Everett Cheetham and another cowboy named
"Slim," after picking up one of the rodeo performers who had been
guilty of a slight error of judgment regarding the agility of the horse
he was riding. It is sung best, as Tex sings it—with the tongue in the
cheek!*

for Bass Voice

There was bul -

lud on the sad-dle___ An' bul - lud all a - ra-ound, An' a great

big pud-dle___ Of bul - lud on the gra-ound.___

2. Oh, a cowboy lay in it,
   All covered with gore,
   An' he never will ride
   Any broncos no more.

3. Oh, pity the cowboy,
   All bul-luddy and red;
   Oh, a bronco fell on him,
   An' mashed in his head.

4. There was bul-lud on the saddle,
   An' bul-lud all araound,
   An' a great big puddle
   Of bul-lud on the graound.

The Cowboy's Christmas Ball

Of all gay dance songs—here is the gayest! Our heartfelt thanks to Tex Ritter, cowboy singer and actor, who passed it on to us. It takes a heap of learning and a deal of singing, but it is immensely worth while.

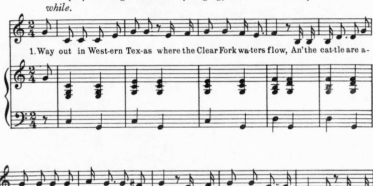

1. Way out in West-ern Tex-as where the Clear Fork wa-ters flow, An' the cat-tle are a-

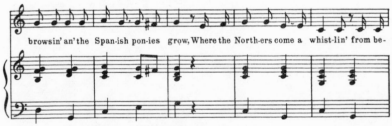

browsin' an' the Span-ish pon-ies grow, Where the North-ers come a whist-lin' from be-

yond the Neu-tral Strip, An' the prai-rie dogs are sneez-in' as if they had the grippe.

Repeat for verses 2 through 7. Then follows the dance inter- polation, on following page.

2. Where the coyotes come a-howlin' 'roun' the ranches after dark,
An' the mockin' birds are singin' to the lovely medder lark;
Where the 'possum an' the badger an' the rattlesnakes abound,
An' the monstrous stars are winkin' o'er a wilderness profound.

3. The town was Anson City, old Jones's county seat,
Where they raised Polled Angus cattle an' wavin' whiskered wheat;
'Twas there, I say, at Anson where the lonely plovers call,
I went to that reception, the Cowboy's Christmas Ball.

4. The music was a fiddle an' a lively tambourine,
An' a viol come imported, by the stage from Abilene.
The room was togged out gorgeous in mistletoe and shawls,
An' the candles flickered festious—whoo!*—aroun' the airy walls.

5. The leader was a feller that come from Swenson's ranch;
They called him "Windy Bill" from Little Dead Man's Branch.
His rig was kinder keerless, long spurs an' high-heeled boots,
An' he had the reputation that comes when a feller shoots.

6. His voice was like the bugle upon the mountain height,
An' his feet was animated, a mighty movin' sight.
Oh, the music started sighin' an' a-wailin' 'roun' the hall.
Hi! it was gettin' active, the Cowboy's Christmas Ball.

7. Then Bill commenced to holler, "Now fellers, shake your pen!
"Lock horns with all them heifers, and rustle 'em like men;
"Doc Hollis down the center, an' twine the ladies chain;
"Van Andrews, pen the fillies in big T Diamond train!"

*Like the wind.

(Interpolation for Dancing)

1. Oh Buf-fa-lo Gal, ain't yuh com-in' out to-night, Com-in' out to-night,
2. Oh meet your old la - dy an' pat 'er on the head, Pat 'er on the head,

com-in' out to-night? Oh ain't yuh, ain't yuh, ain't yuh, ain't yuh

pat 'er on the head, If she don't like whis - key,

com-in' out to-night, An' dance by the light of the moon?___

Give 'er corn bread, Give 'er corn bread in - stead.___

3. Oh, I'll get an-oth-er gal pret-ty as you, Pret-ty as you, pret-ty as you, Oh

I'll get an-oth-er gal pret-ty as you, "Hel-lo, Su - sie Brown!"

4. Flies in the but-ter-milk, two by two, Flies in the but-ter-milk,

two by two, Flies in the but-ter-milk shoo fly, shoo! Skip to my Lou, my

dar - lin'.

5. Oh Buff-a - lo Gal, cain't yuh come out to-night, Come out to-night,

come out to-night? Oh caint yuh, caint yuh, caint yuh, caint you

come out to-night, An' dance by the light of the moon?——

8. The dust riz fast an' fur-ious; we all jes' gal-loped 'round, Till the

scene-ry got so gid-dy that T Bar Dick was downed. We

buck-led to our part-ners, an' told 'em to hold on, Then

shook our hoofs like light-nin' un - til the ear-ly dawn.

Repeat for 2 more verses

9. Don' tell me 'bout cotillions, or germans. No sir-ee!
That whirl at Anson City jes' takes the cake with me.
I'm tired o' lazy shufflin's, of them I've had my fill;
Give me a frontier breakdown backed up by Windy Bill.

10. McAllister ain't nowhere when Windy leads the show;
I've seen 'em both in harness an' so I ought to know.
Oh, Bill, I shan't forget you, an' I oftentimes recall
That lively gaited soiree—wooh!*—the Cowboy's Christmas Ball.

* Like a whoop!

43

The Cowman's Prayer

*The simple prayer of a simple man. Wallace House first sang it to
us—straight from the heart!*

1. O Lord, please lend me now Thine ear. The prayer of a cat-tle man to hear; Per-haps this prayer to You seems strange, But I want You to bless our cat-tle range.

2. The prairie fires, won't You please stop.
   Let thunders roll and water drop.
   It frightens me to see the smoke;
   If it don't stop, I'll go dead broke.

3. O Lord, as You this herd behold,
   It represents a sack of gold;
   I think at least five cents a pound
   Will be the price the whole year round.

4. Just one thing more and then I'm through:
   Instead of one calf, give my cows two!
   I may pray different from other men,
   But I've had my say, and now, Amen.

The Night-Herding Song

The song of the night-herder, singing his herd to sleep, ranks with the most appealing of all songs—cowboy or any other. Written by Harry Stephens, it first appeared in John A. Lomax's original book of Cowboy Songs. The tune as given here, we have never seen or heard anywhere but from Wallace House who taught it to us.

1. Oh say, lit-tle dog-ies, quit your rov-in' a-round, You've wandered and tramped all o-ver this ground. Graze on, lit-tle dog-ies, an' move kind o' slow, An' don't for-ev-er be on the go. Move slow, lit-tle dog-ies, move slow.

46

Much more slowly to the end.

Hi - - Ho, Hi - - Ho, Hey, cat-tle, Hi - Ho.___

2. I've night-herded, trail-herded, cross-herded too,
   But to keep you together, that's what I cain't do;
   My hoss is leg weary an' I'm awful tired,
   But if you git away then I'm sure to get fired.
   Bunch up, little dogies, bunch up.

   Chorus: Hi—Ho, etc.

3. Oh say, little dogies, when you goin' to lay down,
   An' quit this forever a-shiftin' around?
   My legs are a-weary, my seat is all sore;
   Lay down, little dogies, like you laid down before,
   Lay down, little dogies, lay down.

   Chorus: Hi—Ho, etc.

4. Lay still, little dogies, since you have laid down,
   Stretch away out on the big, open ground;
   Snore loud, little dogies, and drown the wild sound
   That will all go away when the day rolls around.
   Lay still, little dogies, lay still.

   Chorus: Hi—Ho, etc.

The Glory Trail

*Tall stories rank high among our favorite folk tales and songs—and
here is one of the tallest: how a cowboy roped a mountain lion and
what befell him as a result. It was written by Badger Clark, as verse;
then turned up some years later among cowboys as a song, in the
version here, as sung to us by Tex Ritter. It is also known as "High
Chin Bob."*

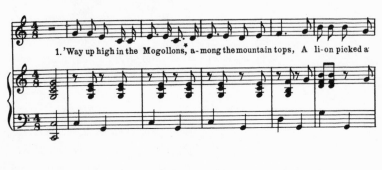

1. 'Way up high in the Mogollons, a-mong the mountain tops, A li-on picked a

year-lin's bones an' licked his thank-ful chops; When who up-on the scent should ride, a

trip-pin' down the slope, But High Chin Bob of sin-ful pride an' maverick-hungry rope.

* Pronounced "Mogoyohns."

48

Chorus *for first four verses*

"Oh glo-ry be to me," says he, "An' fame's un-dy-in' flow'rs; I ride my good top

hoss to day, I'm top hand of the La-zy-J, So Kit-ty-cat, you're ours!"

2. The lion licked his paws so brown, an' dreamed soft dreams of veal,
When High Chin's noose come a-circlin' down an' roped him round his meal;
He yowled quick fury to the world and all the hills yelled back.
That top hoss give a snort an' whirled an' Bob took up the slack.

    Chorus: "Oh glory be to me!" says he. "We'll hit the glory trail.
        "No man has looped a lion's head an' lived to drag the critter dead,
        "Till I shall tell the tale!"

3. 'Way up high in the Mogollons that top hoss done his best,
'Mid whippin' brush an' rattlin' stones from canyon floor to crest;
Up an' down an' round an' cross Bob pounded, weak an' wan,
But pride still glued him to his hoss while glory spurred him on.

    Chorus: "Oh glory be to me!" says he. "This glory trail is rough!
        "But I'll keep this dally round the horn, until the toot of
            judgment morn,
        "Before I'll holler 'nough!"

4. Three suns had rode their circle home, beyond the desert rim,
An' turned their star herds loose to roam the ranges high an' dim;
But whenever Bob, he turned an' hoped the limp remains to find,
A red-eyed lion, belly-roped but healthy, loped behind!

(Additional verses on following page)

49

Chorus: "Oh glory be to me!" says he. "He cain't be drug to death!
"Them heroes that I've read about wus only fools that stuck it out
"To the end of mortal breath!"

5. 'Way up high in the Mogollons, if yuh ever camp there at night,
You'll hear a ruckus among the stones that'll lift your hair with fright;
A cow-hoss comes a-thunderin' by an' a lion trailin' along,
An' a rider bold, with chin on high, sings forth this glory song.

Chorus: (*See music below*)

Hill Folks

During the last quarter-century, our Southern hill folk have been accorded a better understanding of their way of life: their trials and hardships; the effects of their severe, isolated living. And we have learned also what good singers they are, what honest, clear-worded ballads they have written, and with what gusto they sing them!

Cindy

There never was a better square-dance tune than "Cindy." The words are legion; a new stanza and a different version in every county, but the music has the same jig in it everywhere.

1. I wish I was a' ap-ple, a-hangin' on a tree, An' eve-ry time my Cin-dy passed, she'd take a bite o' me. She told me that she loved me, she called me sug-ar plum, She throwed 'er arms a-roun' me, I thought my time had come!

2. Cindy got religion, she'd had it once before.
When she heerd my ol' banjo, she's the first one on the floor.
Cindy took to preachin', she preached around an' 'roun',
She got so full o' glory, she knock' the Preacher down!

Chorus: Git along home, Cindy, Cindy, etc.

3. She took me to the parlor, she cooled me with her fan,
She swore that I'se the purties' thing in the shape of mortal man.
Oh, Cindy in the springtime, Cindy in the fall,
Ef I cain't have my Cindy gal, I'll have no gal at all.

Chorus: Git along home, Cindy, Cindy, etc.

Goin' Down to Town

A favorite of the men driving their load of this and that from the farm to town. The humor is elemental, but the tune sings itself and the words don't get in its way!

1. I used to have a ol' gray hoss, He weigh' ten thou-sand pound;

Ev-'ry tooth was in 'is head, Was eigh-teen inch-es round.

Chorus

I'm a go-in' down to town, I'm a go-in' down to town, I'm a

go - in' down to Lynch-burg town, To car-ry my to-bac-co down.

2. That hoss he had a holler tooth,
   He'd eat ten bushels o' corn.
   Ev'ry time he open' his mouth,
   Two bushels and a half was gone.

   Chorus: I'm a-goin' down to town, etc.

3. I had a little yaller gal;
   I brought her from the South.
   All the fault I had with her,
   She had too big a mouth.

   Chorus: I'm a-goin' down to town, etc.

4. I took her to the blacksmith shop
   To get her mouth made small.
   She opened her mouth to take a breath,
   Swallered blacksmith, shop, and all.

   Chorus: I'm a-goin' down to town, etc.

Ground Hog

Some hunt for sport and some hunt for food, but in our Southern mountains they hunt for both—and make songs about it. Here is a perfect picture of one phase of Kentucky hill-folks' life.

2. Two in a stump an' one in a log,
   Two in a stump an' one in a log,
   Seed 'is nose, Lawd I knew it wuz a hog.
   Ground hog!

3. Sam cocked 'is gun an' Dave pulled the trigger,
   Sam cocked 'is gun an' Dave pulled the trigger,
   But the one killed the hog was ol' Joe Digger.
   Ground hog!

4. Up step' Sal with a snigger an' a grin,
   Up step' Sal with a snigger an' a grin,
   "Whut yuh goin' to do with the ground-hog skin?"
   Ground hog!

5. They put 'im in the pot an' all begun to smile,
   They put 'im in the pot an' all begun to smile,
   They eat that hog before he struck a bile.
   Ground hog!

6. Watch 'im boys, he's about to fall,
   Watch 'im boys, he's about to fall,
   He's eat till 'is pants won't button at all.
   Ground hog!

Mountain Top

Liza Jane was a famous girl. She is most widely sung of any in the Southern mountains; a score of songs and a host of versions. In some she dies, as in the present song; in others she lives on. But always, she is an inspiration!

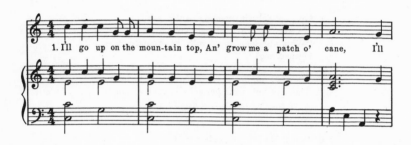

1. I'll go up on the moun-tain top, An' grow me a patch o' cane, I'll

make me a jug o' mo-las-ses too, For to sweet-en lit-tle Li-za Jane.

Chorus

Oh pore Li-za, pore gal, Oh pore Li-za Jane.

Oh pore Li - za, pore gal, She died on the train.

2. Come along, sweet Liza Jane,
   Jes' come along with me;
   We'll go up to the mountain top,
   Some pleasures there to see.

   Chorus: Oh pore Liza, etc.

3. I'll go up on this mountain top,
   Put me out a moonshine still,
   I'll sell you a quart of old moonshine,
   Jes' for a one dollar bill.

   Chorus: Oh pore Liza, etc.

4. I'll eat when I am hung-a-ree,
   An' drink when I am dry,
   An' ef a tree don't fall on me,
   I'll live until I die.

   Chorus: Oh pore Liza, etc.

Colored Folks

It is not on purpose that we have more songs in this section than in any other. It is only because Colored Folks are the most singin' folks; they sing the most and they sing fully as well as the best. And in their songs there is no need to search for origins; they are songs of America!

Alabama Bound

As sung at a party in Colorado in 1910 by one Tom Gregory of Georgia whom the writer had never seen before and has never seen since; nor have we ever seen or heard the song elsewhere.

1. Oh, de boats on de rib-ber___ turn roun' an' roun'___ An' all de wo-men on de Eas' shore yell "Al-a-bam-a boun'!" You want to be lak me, You want to be lak me, Ah got a gal in

In all fairness, we must warn the singer that the rhythm of this song seems, from the printed page, to be confusing. But when the swing of the rhythm is once mastered, it flows naturally with the words.

Birm - in' - ham town, An' one in Ten - nes - see. see.

2. Oh, de boat's up de ribber,
   An' de tide's gone down;
   Believe to mah soul, dat
   She's Alabama boun'.

   Chorus: You want to be lak me, etc.

3. Where wuz you, sweet Mama,
   When de boat w .nt down?
   On de deck, baby, yellin'
   "Alabama boun'!"

   Chorus: You want to be lak me, etc.

4. Got a train in Cairo
   Forty coaches long.
   All I want dat train to do
   Is fetch mah gal along.

   Chorus: You want to be lak me, etc.

5. Doctuh Cook's in town,
   Doctuh Cook's in town.
   He foun' de No'th Pole so doggone cold,
   He's Alabama boun'.

   Chorus: You want to be lak me, etc.

De Blue-Tail Fly

This pestiferous insect has flourished in the South "time out of mind," and this song in his honor seems to date back to Civil War days. It was a favorite with the minstrels—and also with their audiences.

1. When Ah was young Ah use' to wait On Mas-sa an' hand him de plate, An'
pass de bot-tle when he git dry, An' bresh a-way de blue-tail fly.

Chorus
Jim-my crack corn an' Ah don' care, Jim-my crack corn an' Ah don' care,

Jim-my crack corn an' Ah don' care, Ol' Mas-sa's gone a - way.

2. Den atter dinner Massa sleep.
   He bid dis nigger vigil keep,
   An' when he gwine to shut his eye
   He tell me watch de blue-tail fly.

   Chorus: Jimmy crack corn, etc.

3. One day he ride aroun' de farm;
   De flies so numerous dey did swarm.
   One chance' to bite 'im on de thigh.
   De Debble take dat blue-tail fly!

   Chorus: Jimmy crack corn, etc.

4. Dat pony run, he jump, he pitch,
   He tumble Massa in de ditch.
   He died, an' de jury wonder why;
   De verdic' was de blue-tail fly.

   Chorus: Jimmy crack corn, etc.

5. Dey laid 'im under a 'simmon tree;
   His epitaph am dar to see:
   "Beneath dis stone Ah'm fo'ced to lie,
   "All by de means ob de blue-tail fly."

   Chorus: Jimmy crack corn, etc.

6. Ol' Massa gone, now let 'im rest;
   Dey say all t'ings am for de best.
   Ah nebber forget till de day I die,
   Ol' Massa an' dat blue-tail fly.

   Chorus: Jimmy crack corn, etc.

The Boll Weevil

This ballad is not old, as songs go. It was probably written originally during the later 1890's when the boll weevil came over into Texas from Old Mexico. And it has been sung and "built onto" ever since. We venture a prediction that it will be sung as long as cotton is grown in the United States.

Oh, de boll wee-vil am a li'l black bug, Come f'um Mex-i-co, dey

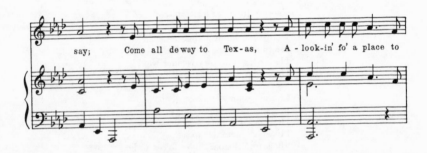

say; Come all de way to Tex-as, A-look-in' fo' a place to

stay; Jes' a-look-in' fo' a home,_____ Jes' a-look-in' fo' a home._____

2. De firs' time Ah see weevil,
   He wus a-settin' on de squar'.
   Next time Ah see de weevil,
   Had all of his fam'ly dar',
   A-lookin' fo' a home,
   Jes' lookin' fo' a home.

3. De farmer say to de weevil
   "What make yo' head so red?"
   An' de weevil say to de farmer,
   "It's a wonder Ah ain' dead,
   "Lookin' fo' a home
   "Jes' lookin' fo' a home."

4. De farmer take de boll weevil
   An' he stick 'im in de hot san'.
   De weevil say, "Dis is mighty hot,
   "But Ah'll stand it lak a man.
   "Dis'll be mah home,
   "It'll be mah home."

5. De farmer take de boll weevil,
   An' he put him in a hunk o' ice,
   An' de weevil say to de farmer,
   "Dis is mighty cool an' nice.
   "It'll be mah home,
   "Dis'll be mah home."

6. De weevil say to de farmer,
   "Yo' better leave me alone;
   "Ah done et all yo' cotton,
   "Now Ah'm startin' on yo' corn.
   "Ah'll have a home,
   "Ah'll have a home."

7. De farmer say to de merchant,
   "We's in a awful fix;
   "De boll weevil done et up all
   de cotton
   "An' he left us only sticks.
   "We'll lose our home,
   "He'll have our home."

8. De weevil say to de doctor,
   "Bettuh th'ow 'way all dem pills.
   "When Ah get th'ough wid de
   farmer,
   "Cain't pay no doctor's bills.
   "Won't have no home,
   "Ah'll have his home."

9. An' de weevil say to de preacher,
   "Jes' close up dat church do'.
   "When Ah get th'ough wid de
   farmer,
   "Cain't pay de preacher no mo'.
   "Won't have no home,
   "Ah'll have his home."

10. An' de weevil say to de farmer,
    "You kin ride in dat Ford
    machine,
    "But when Ah get th'ough wid
    yo' cotton,
    "You cain't buy no gasoline.
    "Won't have no home,
    "Ah'll have yo' home."

The Crawdad Song

A crawdad is a crawfish, good for bait and good for eating—for some folks. This song came to us from Mrs. Fleming of Texas, who sang it in a low, quiet voice, almost sleepily, as if drowsy from the hot sun.

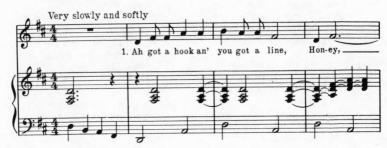

2. See'd a nigger totin' a sack, Honey,
   See'd a nigger totin' a sack, Babe,
   See'd a nigger totin' a sack,
   Had all de crawdad he could pack,
   Honey Babe.

3. Sell mah crawdad three fo' a dime, Honey,
   Sell mah crawdad three fo' a dime, Babe,
   Sell mah crawdad three fo' a dime,
   Kin yo' sell yo's as cheap as mine?
   Honey Babe.

4. Whut you goin' to do when the pond goes dry, Honey?
   Whut you goin' to do when the pond goes dry, Babe?
   Whut you goin' to do when the pond goes dry?
   Sit on de bank an' watch de crawdads die!
   Honey Babe.

5. Dis is de end of mah crawdad song, Honey,
   Dis is de end of mah crawdad song, Babe,
   Dis is de end of mah crawdad song.
   Come on, Honey, better git along,
   Honey Babe.

The Dummy Line

A "dummy" in railroad parlance is a small train running on a short track—an easy target for jeers. This song is part railroad, part "colored folk," part "hobo." The first two stanzas appear in FOLK SONGS OF THE SOUTH by Dorothy Scarborough; the last two, we have only heard, but never seen.

1. Some folks say dat de Dum-my don' run. Come an' lem-me tell you whut de Dum-my done: She lef' St. Louis at half-pas' one, An' she rolled in-to Mem-phis at de set-tin' of de sun.

Chorus

On de Dum-my, — on de Dum-my Line, Rise an' shine. Rise an' shine an'

pay yo' fine, When yuh rid-in' on de Dum-my, on de Dum-my, Dum-my Line.

2. Ah got on de Dummy, didn' have no fare.
   Conductor hollered, "Whut you doin' dere?"
   Ah jumped up an' made fo' de do',
   An' he crack' me on de haid wid a two-by-fo'.

   Chorus: On de Dummy, etc.

3. Ah hopped off de Dummy an' Ah lit on de track,
   Drug mah feet an' scrape' mah back.
   Ah come to life an' slung mah dogs;
   Look fo' sho' lak Ah'm on de hog! *

   Chorus: On de Dummy, etc.

4. Some folks say dat de Dummy don' run;
   Come an' lemme tell you whut de Dummy done.
   She lef' St. Louis at half-past two,
   But Ah walked to Memphis 'fore de Dummy come through!

   Chorus: On de Dummy, etc.

* Down on one's luck.

Nobody's but Mine

Here is a bit, incomplete, but still haunting, and reminiscent of Col-
ored Folks crooning "ad lib" as they work, or walk, or ride—or even
rest. It came to us from Morris Colman; we could wish for more
of it. Notice the strange ending which leaves the tune suspended in
mid-air.

Gwine down to mah shack, Chick-en on mah back, An' it's

no-bod-y's chick-en but mine. Rab-bit up a hol-ler lawg, Got me no

dawg, How Ah'll git 'im out, it's Gawd on-ly knows. Oh Ah'll cut me a

sprout, An' Ah'll twist 'im right out, An' it's no-bod-y's rab-bit but mine.

L.H.

Noonday on de Ribber

Another scrap, but it carries a genial chuckle and a picture of sun-shine and warm lazy water. To us via Bim Mardfin.

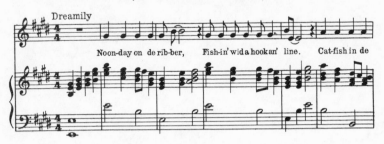

Noon-day on de rib-ber, Fish-in' wid a hook an' line. Cat-fish in de

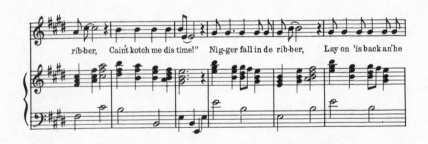

rib-ber, Cain't kotch me dis time!" Nig-ger fall in de rib-ber, Lay on 'is back an' he

wink, Float-in' lak a bub-ble on de wa-ter 'Cause a tub o' grease cain't sink.

Negro Spirituals and Bible Songs

And here speaks man to God, humbly, reverently, as the littlest child to his Father. There are many forms of song, and great songs in every form; but to any listener or singer, white or colored, there is none more moving or more gripping than the Negro Spiritual.

Spirituals in general are too well known and widely sung to need explanation here, or to warrant the duplication of many which appear in other works. We include, therefore, only a few that are less generally known but are no less beautiful.

Here, too, are stories from the Bible—the Old and the New Testament "translated" into song by Colored Folks for themselves. They are almost without exception amusing—but they are never impious. No matter how colloquially phrased, or "comically" twisted, they are fundamentally serious, moral tales.

They have one overwhelming advantage, however, over other serious, moral tales; they are never dull!

All Mah Sins Been Taken Away

That was a good party in 1910. Here is a second song that we find we owe to Tom Gregory.

Not too slowly

1. Ma - ry wove three links of chain, Ma - ry wove three links of

chain, Ma - ry wove three links of chain, Ev -'ry link in Je - sus' name.

All mah sins been tak - en a - way, Tak - en a - way.

2. Ah don' know but Ah's been told,
   Ah don' know but Ah's been told,
   Ah don' know but Ah's been told,
   Gates am pearl an' streets am gold.
      All mah sins been taken away, taken away.

3. Mary weep' an' Martha mourn',
   Mary weep' an' Martha mourn',
   Mary weep' an' Martha mourn',
   Gabriel stood an' blowed 'is horn.
      All mah sins been taken away, taken away.

4. Cain't yuh hear dem hosses' feet?
   Cain't yuh hear dem hosses' feet?
   Cain't yuh hear dem hosses' feet,
   Slippin'—slidin' on de golden street?
      All mah sins been taken away, taken away.

5. Been to de ribbuh an' Ah been baptize',
   Been to de ribbuh an' Ah been baptize',
   Been to de ribbuh an' Ah been baptize',
   Cain't yuh hear how Jesus cries!
      All mah sins been taken away, taken away.

God, He's Gwine to Set Dis World on Fire

A militant spiritual which has been sung in camp meetings, around firesides—and in jails!

1. God,— He's gwine to set dis world on fire,—

God— he's gwine to set dis world on fire, One o' dese days.

God— He's gwine to set dis world on fire— One o' dese days.—

2. Ah'm a-gwine to walk an' talk wid Jesus,
   Ah'm a-gwine to walk an' talk wid Jesus,
   One o' dese days.
   Tell yuh 'bout me* Ah'm gwine to walk an' talk wid Jesus,
   One o' dese days.

3. Ah'm a-gwine to climb up Jacob's ladder,
   Ah'm a-gwine to climb up Jacob's ladder,
   One o' dese days.
   'Cause every round goes higher an' higher,
   One o' dese days.

4. All you sinners gwine turn up missin',
   All you sinners gwine turn up missin',
   One o' dese days.
   Ah'm tellin' yuh now,* you sinners gwine turn up missin',
   One o' dese days.

5. God don't want no coward soldiers,
   God don't want no coward soldiers,
   None o' dese days.
   He wants valiant-hearted soldiers,
   One o' dese days!

6. God, He's gwine to set dis world on fire,
   God, He's gwine to set dis world on fire,
   One o' dese days.
   God, He's gwine to set dis world on fire,
   One o' dese days.

* This phrase covers the first five-eighths of the four-four measure, the same space as taken by the word "God" in the first stanza.

Jesus Goin' to Make Up Mah Dyin' Bed

We have never heard this song except from Wallace House, the most versatile guitarist and Folk Singer we know, who in turn got it from Zora Hurston. It ranks with the most beautiful spirituals.

1. Oh, in mah dy - in' hour, ___ Ah don' want no-bod-y to

moan; All Ah want you to do fo' me Is to fold mah dy-in'

arms. Well, well, well, so Ah kin die eas-y; Well, well, well, so Ah kin die eas-y;

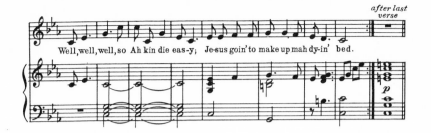

after last verse

Well, well, well, so Ah kin die eas-y; Je-sus goin' to make up mah dy-in' bed.

2. Ah'm a-goin' down to de ribber,
   Stick mah sword up in de sand.
   Goin' to shout, "Mah trouble's over, Lo'd,
   "Ah done made it to de Promis' Land!"
   > Well, well, well, Ah done cross over,
   > Well, well, well, Ah done cross over,
   > Well, well, well, Ah done cross over,
   > Jesus goin' to make up mah dyin' bed.

3. Won't you meet me, Jesus, meet me,
   Won't you meet me in de middle of air,
   An' ef mah wings should fail me, Lo'd,
   Won't you meet me with another pair.
   > Well, well, well, won't you meet me, Jesus,
   > Well, well, well, won't you meet me, Jesus,
   > Well, well, well, won't you meet me, Jesus,
   > Jesus goin' to make up mah dyin' bed.

Satan's a Liar

Here is a spiritual rarely heard—too rarely in our opinion. It "has everything"—melody, rhythm, appealing words—and is easily adapted to chorus singing.

Satan's a liar_____ an' a con-ju'h too;_____ If you

don't watch out,_____ he'll con-ju'h you!_____

Satan's a li-ar an' a conju'h too, If you don't watch out, he'll conju'h you!

82

Oh, I ain' a-gwine-a wor-ry mah Lawd no mo', Ain' a-gwine-a wor-ry mah Lawd no mo!

2. Gwine-a go tuh Heav'n—on a Angel's wing,
   An' when Ah git dere—you'll hear me sing!
   Gwine-a go tuh Heav'n on a Angel's wing,
   An' when Ah git dere how Ah will sing!

   Chorus: Oh, Ah ain' a-gwine-a worry, etc.

3. When Ah git tuh Heav'n—gwine-a set me down,
   Gwine-a put on mah wings—an' starry crown,
   When Ah git tuh Heav'n, gwine-a set me down,
   Gwine-a put on mah wings an' starry crown.

   Chorus: Oh, Ah ain' a-gwine-a worry, etc.

'Way Over in the Promised Land

A song of the pioneers, borrowed possibly from the Negroes. It has been called by Sandburg a "white man's spiritual"; another favorite for choruses.

1. Where O where is old E - li - jah? Where O where is old E - li - jah?
He went up in a fie - ry chariot, He went up in a fie - ry chariot,

Where O where is old E - li - jah? 'Way o -ver in the prom-ised land.
He went up in a fie - ry char-iot, 'Way o -ver in the prom-ised land.

Chorus

By and by we'll go and see him, By and by we'll go and see him.

By and by we'll go and see him, 'Way o-ver in the prom-ised land.

2. Where O where are the Hebrew children?
   Where O where are the Hebrew children?
   Where O where are the Hebrew children?
   'Way over in the promised land.
   > They went up in a fiery furnace,
   > They went up in a fiery furnace,
   > They went up in a fiery furnace,
   > > 'Way over in the promised land.

   Chorus: By and by we'll go and see them, etc.

3. Where O where is the bad boy Absalom?
   Where O where is the bad boy Absalom?
   Where O where is the bad boy Absalom?
   'Way over in the promised land.
   > He went up on the spear of Joab,
   > He went up on the spear of Joab,
   > He went up on the spear of Joab,
   > > 'Way over in the promised land.

   Chorus: By and by we'll go and see him, etc.

4. Where O where is poor old Daniel?
   Where O where is poor old Daniel?
   Where O where is poor old Daniel?
   'Way over in the promised land.
   > He went down in a den of lions,
   > He went down in a den of lions,
   > He went down in a den of lions,
   > > 'Way over in the promised land.

   Chorus: By and by we'll go and see him, etc.

Climb to Glory

Here is one of the gayest (but with a broad vein of piety) as sung to us by Fred Melcher, to whom apologies are herewith tendered for such changes from his rendition as have crept in!

1. Oh, de Lo'd says to No-ah, "It's gwine-a be a lit-tle flood-y, flood-y!" De

Lo'd says to No-.ah, "It's gwine-a be a lit-tle flood-y, flood-y, Get yo'

chillen out ob de mud-dy, mud-dy, Chillen___ of de Lo'd." Rise an' shine, an'

gib God de glo-ry, glo-ry, Rise an' shine, an' gib God de glo-ry, glo-ry,

Rise an' shine an' climb to glo-ry, glo-ry, Chillen ___ ob de Lo'd! ___

2. Noah, Noah built him an Arky, Arky,
   Noah, Noah built him an Arky, Arky,
   Built it out of hickory barky, barky,
   Chillen ob de Lo'd.

   Chorus: Rise an' shine, etc.

3. De animals dey clumb on boa'd, two by twoy, twoy,
   De animals dey clumb on boa'd, two by twoy, twoy,
   De elephants and de kangarooy, -rooy,
   Chillen ob de Lo'd.

   Chorus: Rise an' shine, etc.

4. Jacob stood at de foot ob de ladder, ladder,
   Jacob stood at de foot ob de ladder, ladder,
   Ol' St. Peter says, "Whut're you atter, atter,
   "Chillen ob de Lo'd!"

   Chorus: Rise an' shine, etc.

Dese Bones Gwine to Rise Again

Genesis in song, simple and understandable, as taught to darky children—and perhaps many grownups—for generations.

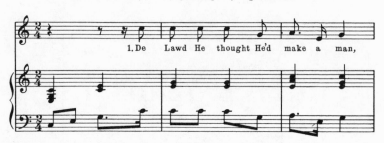

1. De Lawd He thought He'd make a man,

Dese bones gwine to rise a-gain. Made him out o' mud an' a

lit-tle bit o' san', Dese bones gwine to rise a-gain. Tuck a rib f'um

Ad-am's side, Dese bones gwine to rise a-gain. Made Miss Eve fo' to

be his bride, Dese bones gwine to rise a - gain.

Chorus

Ah knows it, brud-der, Yes Ah knows it, brud-der,

'Deed Ah knows it, brud-der, Dese bones gwine to rise a - gain.—

(Additional verses on following page.)

Live a-Humble

*And again we have to thank Tom Gregory, this time for a Bible
story which we have not seen elsewhere. Our only regret is that we
could remember no more!*

1. Ol' man Ad-am were de fus' man in-vent-ed; He live' all a - lone, but he

warn' contented. 'Long come Eve an' dey had a bat-tle, Ad-am sent Eve out to

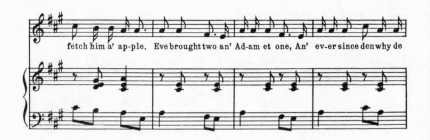

fetch him a' ap-ple. Eve brought two an' Ad-am et one, An' ev-er since den why de

2. Put 'em in a garden rich an' fair,
　　Dese bones gwine to rise again,
　But touch one tree dey mus' not dare,
　　Dese bones gwine to rise again.
　Sarpint he come 'roun' de trunk,
　　Dese bones gwine to rise again,
　At Miss Eve his eye he wunk,
　　Dese bones gwine to rise again.

　Chorus: Ah knows it, brudder, etc.

3. Adam, he come a-prowlin' 'roun',
　　Dese bones gwine to rise again,
　Spied some peelin's on de groun',
　　Dese bones gwine to rise again.
　Fust he tuk a little slice,
　　Dese bones gwine to rise again,
　Smack' his lips an' say 'twus nice,
　　Dese bones gwine to rise again.

　Chorus: Ah knows it, brudder, etc.

4. De Lawd He spoke with a mighty voice,
　　Dese bones gwine to rise again,
　Shuck de Heavens to de joists!
　　Dese bones gwine to rise again.
　"Y' et Mah apples, Ah believe?"
　　Dese bones gwine to rise again.
　"No Sir, Lawd, but Ah spec' 'twus Eve!"
　　Dese bones gwine to rise again.

　Chorus: Ah knows it, brudder, etc.

trou-ble be-gun. So live a-hum-ble, Live a-hum-ble, Hum-ble yo' se'f to de Lo'd.

Ol' man No-ah, hunt-in' in de dark, He foun' him a ham-mer an' he

built him a' ark. A - long come de an - i - mules, two by two; Here

come a hip-po-pot-a-mus an' a kee-kan-ga-roo; So live a-

hum-ble, Live a - hum-ble, Humble yo' se'f to de Lo'd.

Jo - nah went a sail-in', 'thout an-y or-ders. A - long come de waves an'

dash him in de wa-ters. A - long come de whale an' swaller Jo-nah up; He sail'

'round fo' three days an' three nights. Whale's stom-ach be-

The Hoedown

There are no gayer, livelier tunes than the hoedowns, breakdowns, and reels which flourished in farm and log-cabin communities before the coming of the automobile, the radio, or even the telephone.

The beat was given by the fiddler's tapping foot; the formations dictated by the "Caller." For this type of American Folk Song, whether the singer be white or colored, the voice and the feet work together. Those of sound wind can sing as they dance; others can sing or dance. But the sounds of voices and "stomping" are inseparable.

A country dance was an occasion for several days' holiday: a day to get there—all night for the dance—a day to get back—and perhaps a day to catch up on sleep!

Bile Dem Cabbage Down

To be sung to a banjo, fiddle or guitar, and shuffling and stamping feet. The words may be found in Dorothy Scarborough's On the Trail of the Negro Folk Song; *the tune—nowhere that we know of.*

1. Mas-sa had a old gray roos-ter, Use-tuh crow fo' day. A-

long come a har-ri-cane, An' blow dat chicken a-way.

Chorus

Bile dem cab-bage down, Bile dem cab-bage down,

Stop dat fool-ish - ness I say, An' bile dem cab-bage down.

2. Wish Ah had a li'l tin box
   To keep mah sweetheart in.
   Ah'd take her out an' kiss her,
   An' put her back ag'in.

   Chorus: Bile dem cabbage down, etc.

3. Wish Ah had a needle an' thread,
   Fine as Ah could sew.
   Ah'd sew mah sweetheart to mah side,
   An' down de road we'd go.

   Chorus: Bile dem cabbage down, etc.

4. Some folks say de Debbil's dead
   An' buried in a shoe,
   But Ah see'd de Debbil t'other day,
   An' he look' jes' good as new.

   Chorus: Bile dem cabbage down, etc.

5. If Ah had a scoldin' wife,
   Ah'd whop her sho's yo' born;
   Ah'd hitch her to a double plow,
   An' make her plow mah corn.

   Chorus: Bile dem cabbage down, etc.

Cl'ar de Kitchen

A Negro dance melody sung in Virginia, Florida, South Carolina, West Virginia—and all parts south. Possibly originated by the minstrels, according to Dorothy Scarborough.

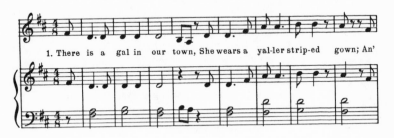

1. There is a gal in our town, She wears a yal-ler strip-ed gown; An'

when she walks de streets a-roun', De holler of her foot makes a hole in de groun'.

Chorus

Ol' folks, young folks, cl'ar de kitch-en! Ol' folks, young folks,

98

cl'ar de kitch-en, For de ol' Vir - gin-ny Reel! ___

2. As Ah was walkin' up Three Chop Road,
   Ah met a terrapin an' a toad,
   An' every time de toad would jump,
   Terrapin dodge' behin' a stump.

   Chorus: Ol' folks, young folks, etc.

3. Jay bird settin' on a swingin' limb,
   He wink' at me an' Ah wink' at him.
   Ah picked up a rock an' hit him on de chin.
   "Look heah, Man, don't yuh do dat ag'in!"

   Chorus: Ol' folks, young folks, etc.

4. Bull frog dressed in sojer's clo's,
   Went to de field to shoot some crows.
   De crows smell powder an' fly away.
   Bull frog mighty mad dat day.

   Chorus: Ol' folks, young folks, etc.

Mah Mammy Stoled a Cow

A few stanzas of a dance song that could well be endless; a good caller could (and many doubtless did) make them up until the dancers were exhausted!

1. Steal up, young la-dies, Mah mam-my stoled a cow.

Steal up, mah dar-lin' chile, Mah Mam-my stoled a cow.

Chorus

Stole dat cow in Bal-ti-mo', Mah Mam-my stoled a cow,

Stole dat cow in Bal - ti - mo'. Mah Mam-my stoled a cow.

2. Steal up and take yo' turn,
   Mah mammy stoled a cow,
   Steal up and take yo' turn,
   Mah mammy stoled a cow.

   Chorus: Stole dat cow in Baltimo', etc.

3. Steal up an' make a bow,
   Mah mammy stoled a cow,
   Steal up an' make a bow,
   Mah mammy stoled a cow.

   Chorus: Stole dat cow in Baltimo', etc.

4. Steal all 'roun', don' slight no one,
   Mah mammy stoled a cow,
   Steal all 'roun', don' slight no one,
   Mah mammy stoled a cow.

   Chorus: Stole dat cow in Baltimo', etc.

'T Aint Gwine Rain No Mo'

*Here is a dance tune—a reel—singable by one, a few, or a thousand,
which also goes back to slavery days. The tune and words have been
used for more or less recent "popular" songs.*

Dance Song

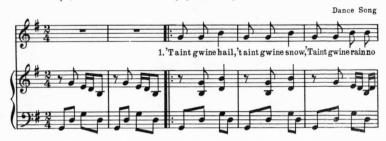

1. 'T aint gwine hail, 't aint gwine snow, 'T aint gwine rain no

mo'; Steal up, ev-'ry-bod-y, 'T aint gwine rain no mo'.

[To be used occasionally between some of the verses only — violin, piano or whistling —
ad lib during the dance.

2. Ol' cow died at de mouth of de
      branch,
   'T aint gwine rain no mo';
   De buzzards held a public dance,
   'T aint gwine rain no mo'.

3. What did de blackbird say to the
      crow?
   'T aint gwine rain no mo';
   'T aint gwine hail an' it aint gwine
      ·snow,
   'T aint gwine rain no mo'.

4. Pick up co'n in a begum hat,
   'T aint gwine rain no mo';
   Ol' Massa grumble if you eat
      much o' dat,
   'T aint gwine rain no mo'.

5. Two, two an' round up fo',
   'T aint gwine rain no mo';
   Lead yo' lady roun' de flo',
   'T aint gwine rain no mo'.

6. Rabbit skip' de garden gate,
   'T aint gwine rain no mo';
   Picked a bean an' pulled his
      freight,
   'T aint gwine rain no mo'.

7. Rabbit et a turnip top,
   'T aint gwine rain no mo';
   Off he went a-lippity-hop
   'T aint gwine rain no mo'.

8. Rabbit hidin' 'hind a pine,
   'T aint gwine rain no mo';
   Had one eye shut an' t'other eye
      blin',
   'T aint gwine rain no mo'.

9. Bake dem biscuits good an' brown,
   'T aint gwine rain no mo';
   Swing yo' partner round an' round
      —an' round—an' round,
   'T aint gwine rain no mo'.

Who Mou'n fo' Me?

*A rapid-fire, quick-step dance with no particular sequence or story;
just words, plaintive and inconsequential, and a tune that sets all feet
in motion.*

1. Rid-in' in de buggy, Miss Mary Jane, Miss Mary Jane, Miss Mary Jane,

Rid-in' in de bug-gy, Miss Ma - ry Jane, Ah'm a   long ways from home.

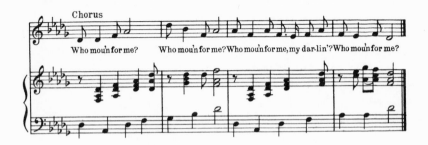

Chorus

Who mou'n for me?   Who mou'n for me? Who mou'n for me, my dar-lin'? Who mou'n for me?

2. Ah got a gal in Baltimo',
   In Baltimo',
   In Baltimo',
   In Baltimo',
   Ah got a gal in Baltimo'
   An' she's three stories high.

   Chorus: Who mou'n fo' me, etc.

3. Sally got a house
   In Baltimo',
   In Baltimo',
   In Baltimo',
   Sally got a house in Baltimo'
   An' it's full o' chicken pie.

   Chorus: Who mou'n fo' me, etc.

Run, Nigger, Run

A dance tune—reel or hoedown—of slavery days—pre-Civil War.
It is a typical story of suffering told with a grin.

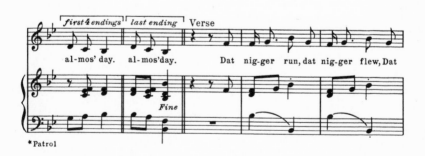

*Patrol

nig - ger lost his wed-din' shoe, He run to de rib - ber but he couldn' get a - cross, He jump' on a hog an' thought it wuz a hoss - Oh

Chorus: Run, nigger, run, etc.

2. Dis nigger run, he run his bes',
   He stuck his head in a hornet nes',
   He jump' de fence an' run fru de paster;
   White man run, but nigger run faster.

   Chorus: Run, nigger, run, etc.

3. Some folks say dat a nigger won't steal,
   But Ah kotch one in mah co'n-fiel';
   He run to de eas', he run to de wes',
   He run 'is head in de hornet nes', Oh

   Chorus: Run, nigger, run, etc.

4. Mah ol' Missus prommus me
   Dat when she die she sot me free;
   But she done dead dis many year ago,
   An' here Ah'm a-hoein' de same ol' row! Oh

   Chorus: Run, nigger, run, etc.

107

5. Ah'm a-hoein' 'cross, Ah'm a-hoein' 'roun',
   Ah'm a-cleanin' up some mo' new groun',
   Whar Ah lif' so hard, Ah lif' so free,
   Mah sins rise up in front o' me! Oh

   Chorus: Run, nigger, run, etc.

6. But some o' dese days mah time'll come,
   Ah'll hear dat bugle, Ah'll hear dat drum,
   Ah'll see dem armies a-marchin' 'long,
   Ah'll lif' mah head an' jine de song! Oh

   Chorus: Run, nigger, run, etc.

The Other Side of the Law

Wealth and poverty set people apart. In America, railroad tracks have become a symbol of the dividing line between the Best people and the Others. But the Great Divide is deeper and wider than money. It is The Law. Here are a few songs that have come over the prison walls.

Billy the Kid

*First came the pioneers and then the outlaws, before the frontiers
became regularized into orderly living. We have many songs of
"bad men" but of none more notorious than Billy the Kid.*

1. I'll sing you a true song of Bil-ly the

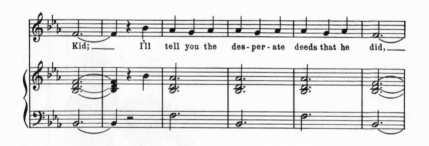

Kid;___ I'll tell you the des-per-ate deeds that he did,___

___'Way out in New Mex-i-co, long, long a-go,___ When a

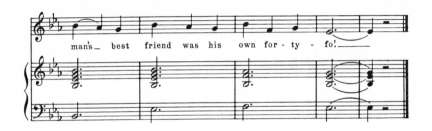

man's__ best friend was his own for - ty - fo.'____

2. When Billy the Kid was a very young lad,
   In old Silver City he went to the bad.
   'Way out in the West with a gun in each han',
   At the age of twelve years he had killed his first man.

3. Oh, Mexican ladies play guitars and sing,
   They sing about Billy, their Boy Bandit King;
   How, ere his young manhood had reached its sad en',
   Had a notch in his pistol for twenty-one men.

4. 'Twas on the same night when poor Billy died,
   He said to his friends, "I am not satisfied.
   "Oh, twenty-one men I have put bullets through,
   "An' Sheriff Pat Garrett must make twenty-two!"

5. I tell you how Billy the Kid met his fate:
   The bright moon was shinin', the hour was late;
   Shot down by Pat Garrett who once was his friend,
   The young outlaw's life had now reached its sad end.

6. There's many a man with a face fine and fair,
   Who starts out in life with a chance to be square;
   But just like poor Billy, he wanders astray,
   And loses his life in the very same way.

The Midnight Special

*"Midnight Special" was the name given by prisoners for a pardon.
There are a number of American "jail songs," but few more poign-
ant than this.*

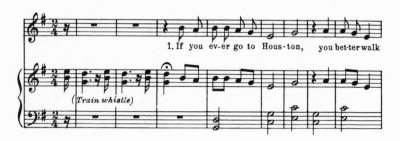

1. If you ev-er go to Hous-ton, you bet-ter walk

right, — You bet-ter not gam-ble, an' you bet-ter not fight, — Or the

sheriff will ar-rést you, He'll take you down, An' the Judge will sentence you,

an' you're jailhouse boun'.— Let the Midnight Spe-cial shine its light up-on me — Oh, twen-ty long years — in the pen-i-ten-tia-ry. —

2. Yonder comes Miss Rosy. Tell me how do you know?
   By the color of her apron an' the dress she wore.
   Umberella on her shoulder—piece o' paper in 'er han',
   She says to de Captain, "Ah wants mah man!"

   Chorus: Let the Midnight Special, etc.

Willie the Weeper

*Willie had his beginnings a long time ago, we believe in San Fran-
cisco. He underwent a curious metamorphosis a few years ago, and
emerged from Tin Pan Alley as "Minnie the Moocher," changed as
to sex, words, and music. We are indebted for the original to Mrs.
Dorothy Rolph.*

1. Oh, hark to the sto-ry of Wil-lie the Weep-er, Wil-lie the
Weep-er was a chim-me-ney sweep-er; Had a hop hab-it, an' he had it bad.
Lis-ten to the sto-ry of a dream he had, An' of a dream he had.

2. He went into a joint—it was late one night—
   Where he knew the lights would be a-burnin' bright,
   An' he says to the Chink to give 'im some dope,
   So the Chink laid out a tray of hops to smoke,
           A tray of hops to smoke.

3. He rolled hisself some five or six pills,
   That he knew would cure up all 'is pains an' ills,
   An' he laid 'imself down an' he went to sleep,
   An' he dreamt he was a-sailin' on the ocean deep,
           Upon the ocean deep.

4. He started playin' poker when he lef' the land,
   An' he won a million dollars on the very firs' hand.
   An' when he seen that the guys was broke,
   He laid 'imself down an' took another smoke,
           An' took another smoke.

5. He went to a place that they called Siam,
   An' he beat the King with a royal-flush han'.
   From the King of Siam he won a million or more,
   An' he went to Monte Carlo when the King got sore,
           When the King got sore.

6. In Monte Carlo he played roulette;
   Couldn' lose a nickel had 'e played on a bet.
   An' when he saw that the bank was broke,
   He bought a million dollars' worth of hops to smoke,
           Worth of hops to smoke.

7. He went to Paris, France, to buy up all the wine,
   For a whole carload 'e paid a measly dime.
   He bought a ruby bush an' a diamond tree,
   For to tote back home to 'is family,
           To 'is family.

8. Oh, that was the story of Willie the Weeper,
   Willie the Weeper was a chimmeney sweeper,
   Had a hop habit an' he had it bad,
   An' that was the story of a dreamy lad,
           An' of a dream he had.

The Penitentiary Blues

A song from Leavenworth prison that is reminiscent of "The Briary Bush," an old English song that exists in many forms in the United States. For the words and music below, which we have never seen in print, we have to thank Earl Humphreys. Popular songs within the last twenty-five years have made use of the melody below, but we believe that it originated with these words.

For Men's Voices

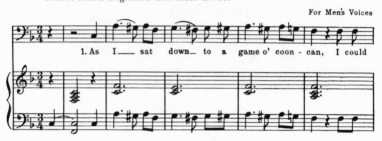

1. As I sat down to a game o' coon-can, I could

hard-ly hold my han' I got to think-in' of the

wo-man I loved, She run a-way with an-oth-er man.

2. I went down to the depot;
        The train was rollin' by.
   I looked in the window, saw the woman I love,
        An' I hung down my head to cry.

3. My mammy's dead in the cold, cold ground,
        My dad he's far away.
   My sister married a gamblin' man,
        An' that's why I'm this way.

4. I climbed on board that east-boun' train
        An' walked right down the aisle,
   An' then I pulled my forty-four gun
        And shot that dark-faced guy.

5. The night was dark and stormy,
        It shore did look like rain,
   I ain't got a friend in the whole, wide world
        An' nobody knows my name.

6. "Oh, Judge—oh, Judge—Oh, Mister Judge,
        "What are you goin' to do with me?"
   "If the jury finds you guilty, poor boy,
        "I'll send you to the penitentiary."

7. The jury found me guilty;
        The clerk he wrote it down;
   They handed me over to the Sheriff man,
        An' I'm Leavenworth, Kansas, boun'.

8. I thought I heard a woman cry,
        She was only singing a song—
   "Someday, someday, some rainy day,
        "You'll be free someday 'fore long."

9. "Won't you wait just a minute, Mr. Hangman,
        "Won't you wait a little while?
   "I think I see my dear old dad,
        "An' he's come for many a mile."

10. "Oh, Dad, did you bring me any silver?
        "Oh, Dad, did you bring me any gold?
    "Or did you come down just to see your boy hung—
        "Hung on the hangman's pole?"

(Additional verses on following page)

117

11. "My boy, I didn' bring you no silver,
     "My boy, I didn' bring you no gold.
   "I jus' come down for to see my boy hung—
     "Hung on the hangman's pole!"

12. "Won't you wait just a minute, Mr. Hangman,
     "Won't you wait a little while?
   "I think I see my sweetheart dear,
     "And she's come for many a mile."

13. "Oh, Gal, did you bring me any silver?
     "Oh, Gal, did you bring me any gold?
   "Or did you come down just to see your boy hung—
     "Hung on the hangman's pole?"

14. "My boy, I brought you some silver,
     "My boy, I brought you some gold.
   "I didn' come down just to see my boy hung—
     "Hung on the hangman's pole."

15. She led me to her parlor,
     An' took me by the hand,
   An' then she cried with all her might,
     "I love my highwayman!"

A Little Nonsense—Now and Then

Just foolishness—but so hilarious! And just as useful as it is harm-less. Here one laughs only at oneself and with others.

The Crazy Dixie

No very popular song can go very long without being parodied; and the gay "zip" of Dixie's tune has made it a constant invitation to amateur versifiers. Below is as absurd a collection of strung-together words as we have ever seen. (Part of it appears also in Sandburg.) Thanks are due to Prof. Herbert Brucker of the School of Journalism, Columbia University, for a substantial portion.

1. I had a hoss, his name was Bill, And when he ran, he couldn't stand still, He ran a-way, one day, And al-so I ran with him.

2. He ran so hard he couldn't stop;
   He ran into a barber shop;
   He fell exhausted, with his teeth,
   In the barber's left shoulder.

3. Oh, I went out into the woods last year,
   To hunt for beer, and not for deer.
   I am—I ain't—
   A great sharpshootress.

4. At shooting birds I am a beaut;
   There is no bird I cannot shoot,
   In the eye, in the ear,
   In the nose, in the fingertips.

5. In Frisco Bay there lives a whale,
   And she eats pork chops by the bale,
   By the hat box, by the pill box,
   By the hogshead and schooner.

6. Her name is Lena; she's a peach,
   But don't leave food within her reach,
   Or babies, or nursemaids,
   Or chocolate ice-cream sodas.

7. She loves to laugh and, when she smiles,
   You just see teeth for miles and miles,
   And tonsils, and spare ribs,
   And things too fierce to mention.

8. She knows no games, so when she plays,
   She rolls her eyes for days and days,
   And vibrates, and yodels,
   And breaks the Ten Commandments!

9. Oh, what can you do in a case like that,
   Oh, what can you do but stamp on your hat,
   Or on an eggshell, or a toothbrush,
   Or anything that's helpless.

Kafoozelum

*An old college favorite; to our mind, better than many more popular
songs of that class. The chorus lends itself majestically to "expan-
siveness"!*

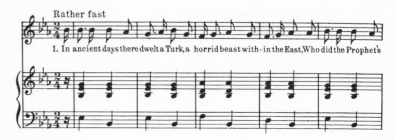

1. In ancient days there dwelt a Turk, a horrid beast with-in the East, Who did the Prophet's

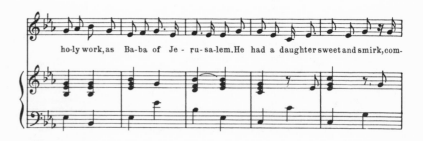

ho-ly work, as Ba-ba of Je-ru-sa-lem. He had a daughter sweet and smirk, com-

plexion fair and dark blue hair, With naught about her like a Turk, ex-cept her name, Ka-foo-zel-um.

Chorus

Oh, Ka - foo - zel - um, Ka - foo - zel - um, Ka - foo - zel - um!

Oh, Ka - foo - zel - um, the daugh-ter of the Ba - ba.

2. A youth resided near to she; his name was Sam, a perfect lamb,
   He came of ancient pedigree descended from Methusalem.
   He drove a trade and prospered well, in skins of cats and ancient hats;
   And, ringing at the Baba's bell, he saw and loved Kafoozelum. (Chorus)

3. If Sam had been a Mussulman, he might have sold the Baba old,
   And with a verse of Alcoran, have managed to bamboozle 'um;
   But, oh dear no! he tried to scheme, pass'd one night late the area gate,
   And stole up to the Turk's hareem, to carry off Kafoozelum. (Chorus)

4. The Baba was about to smoke, his slaves rushed in with horrid din,
   "Marshalla! Dogs your house have broke, come down, my lord, and toozelum!"
   The Baba wreathed his face in smiles, came down the stair and witnessed there,
   A gentleman in three old tiles,* a-kissing of Kafoozelum. (Chorus)

5. The pious Baba said no more than twenty pray'rs, but went upstairs,
   And took a bowstring from a drawer, and came back to Kafoozelum.
   The maiden and the youth he took, and choked them both, and nothing loath,
   Together pitched them in the Brook of Kedron, near Jerusalem. (Chorus)

6. And still, the ancient legend goes, when day is done from Lebanon,
   And when the Eastern moonlight throws a shadow on Jerusalem;
   Between the wailing of the cats, a sound there falls from ruin'd walls,
   A ghost is seen in three old hats, a-kissing of Kafoozelum. (Chorus)

* Old New York for "hat."

123

Jonathan Smith

And here is American history taught the easy way—by song. It is a Modern, written by Prof. Karl N. Llewellyn (Betts Professor of Law at Columbia University) who I know places Folk Songs almost, if not quite, on a par with The Law as a factor in human life!

The reader who is interested in the effects of singers on songs will find it amusing to compare the words below (which were learned by ear in the 1920's) with the words as printed in Dr. Llewellyn's book of verse, PUT IN HIS THUMB (Century Co., 1931). He will find changes of phrase that have crept in quite unconsciously, in the singing; which is exactly what happens to all Folk Songs. In this way, "versions" are born!

Melody of "When Johnny Comes Marching Home."

1. Three hun-dred years a - go or more, so runs the an-cient

tale,___ A cap-tain sailed from Eng-land's shore, and

he was stout and hale.— He'd fought the French and he'd fought the Dutch, the Rus-sians and Prus-sians and Squus-sians and such, And when he'd fin-ished, they need-ed a crutch, for his name was Jon-a-than Smith.

Chorus

His name was Jon-a-than, Jon-a-than, Jon-a-than, Jon-a-than, Jon-a-than Smith.

(Additional verses on following page)

2. The crowd he was with, both young and old, were gentlemen neat and fine.
The gentlemen came to hunt for gold, and eager to own a mine,
But they didn't like work, they hated the dirt, they quit the minute the blisters hurt.
Yet they hollered for double dessert, not like Jonathan Smith.

Chorus: Not like Jonathan, Jonathan, etc.

3. They feasted and piled the pyrites high, till their glimmering hopes were doomed.
The food was getting extremely shy while the gentlemen glumped and gloomed.
But Jonathan Smith pitched into the crew and found each gentleman jobs to do,
With nothing to eat till the work was through, for his name was Jonathan Smith.

Chorus: His name was Jonathan, Jonathan, etc.

4. Now when the Injuns heard his fame, they streaked their war paint on,
And while old John was stalking game, the tribe was stalking John.
Well, Jonathan fought as he'd fought before, and settled the hash of a dozen or more,
But a war club caught him across the jore, and they captured Jonathan Smith.

Chorus: They captured Jonathan, Jonathan, etc.

5. And now by all the Injun laws, the gauntlet he had to run.
The Chieftain's daughter and all the squaws came out to see the fun.
Lined up in an alley, the Indians stood, brandishing clubs and yelling for blood,
And Jonathan thought that his name was mud, instead of Jonathan Smith.

Chorus: Instead of Jonathan, Jonathan, etc.

6. The first one aimed a terrible swat, but John was never a dub;
He sank his fist in the Injun's pot and grabbed away his club.
And, oh, boy! but the fight was hot as he battled his way to the end of the lot.
I'll tell you he gave as good as he got, did Captain Jonathan Smith.

Chorus: Did Captain Jonathan, Jonathan, etc.

7. But Captain John was all alone, so they downed him with a rush;
They placed his head on a likely stone and got it ready to squush.
But Pocahontas, the Chieftain's daughter, well—maybe she took to him more'n
    she oughter,
And forgot everything that her mother had taught'er for love of Jonathan Smith.

Chorus: For love of Jonathan, Jonathan, etc.

8. She leapt like a doe on Captain John, his cheek to hers she drew,
"Lay on, if you must," she panted; "lay on, but you'll have to squush me too!"
So she pestered the Indians John to save, and they let him go rather than hear her rave,
And it pays to be handsome as well as brave, like Captain Jonathan Smith.

Chorus: Like Captain Jonathan, Jonathan, etc.

Index of First Lines

Index of Titles

Songs of American Folks